The ABCs
of Learning the Bible

by Dwayne Douglas

Illustrated by Arsal

Copyright © 2020 Dwayne Douglas.

All rights reserved. No part of this publication may be reproduced, distributed, or transmitted in any form or by any means, including photocopying, recording, or other electronic or mechanical methods, without the prior written permission of the publisher, except in the case of brief quotations embodied in critical reviews and certain other noncommercial uses permitted by copyright law. For permission requests, write to the publisher, addressed "Attention: Permissions Coordinator," at the address below.

ISBN: 978-1-7333140-1-5 (hardcover)
978-1-7333140-3-9 (paperback)

Any references to historical events, real people, or real places are used fictitiously. Characters and places are products of the illustrator's imagination.

Illustrated by Arsal
Edited by Rochelle Douglas

Writer.TDDouglas Publishing

Writer.TDDouglas
PO Box 72
Smyrna, TN 37167-9998

Special thanks to the following preachers…

Anthony Walker

Charles Taylor

Chris Whitaker

David Ricks

David Young

Ernest Lemon

Gordon Newsome, Sr.

James Emerson (R.I.P.)

Joseph W. Walker III

Kenneth Fleming, Jr.

Lovell Hayes

THANK YOU

This book is starting with a sir and then it will address the madam.

It is starting with a sir because God started with Adam.

Now the second letter is why this book was written, so don't forget to open one and look.

This book was written to advise you of people in the Bible, a very important book.

The Bible is full of many stories, all which tell of the truth.

Some about individuals, others about couples - like Boaz and Ruth.

The Bible will help you learn not to take your blessings for granted, because God can always turn the table.

One minute can be good, but it can also change - like Cain did to Abel.

Life as a Christian will help you smile, although there are times you will frown.

Being a Christian doesn't mean it will always be good, because anybody can let you down.

Sometimes problems will jump into your life, sometimes they will enter by creeping.

Look how Delilah changed life for a man while he was sleeping.

It is good to be around other people, that is why God allowed Eve to become Adam's wife.

But don't allow others to make bad decisions that will not help you in life.

However, people will do as they please, and their views will surely be tested.

Someone will probably judge you like Felix did Paul when he was arrested.

If you sin, you can be forgiven. There is a way to come back from your loss.

But don't take my word, read about how God let Jesus die on the cross.

You will then know the truth and will see I'm not a liar.

God could have saved Jesus like Hananiah was saved from that fire.

You should never question God, even if something happens and you think it is not nice.

Without questioning, Abraham was about to give up Isaac because he was told that his son he needed to sacrifice.

As a person of God, wear your cross daily and just know your role.

Remember that it is God and not you in control.

Should you get baptized? That is an easy question. I know you have answered some harder.

Just read the Bible, John baptized in water.

Never be afraid to face big challenges that may look like a brick wall.

Look how David became King or how he made big Goliath fall.

Saving Daniel's three friends was real and not an illusion or trick by a magician.

God took care of them without burns, so they didn't need Luke the physician.

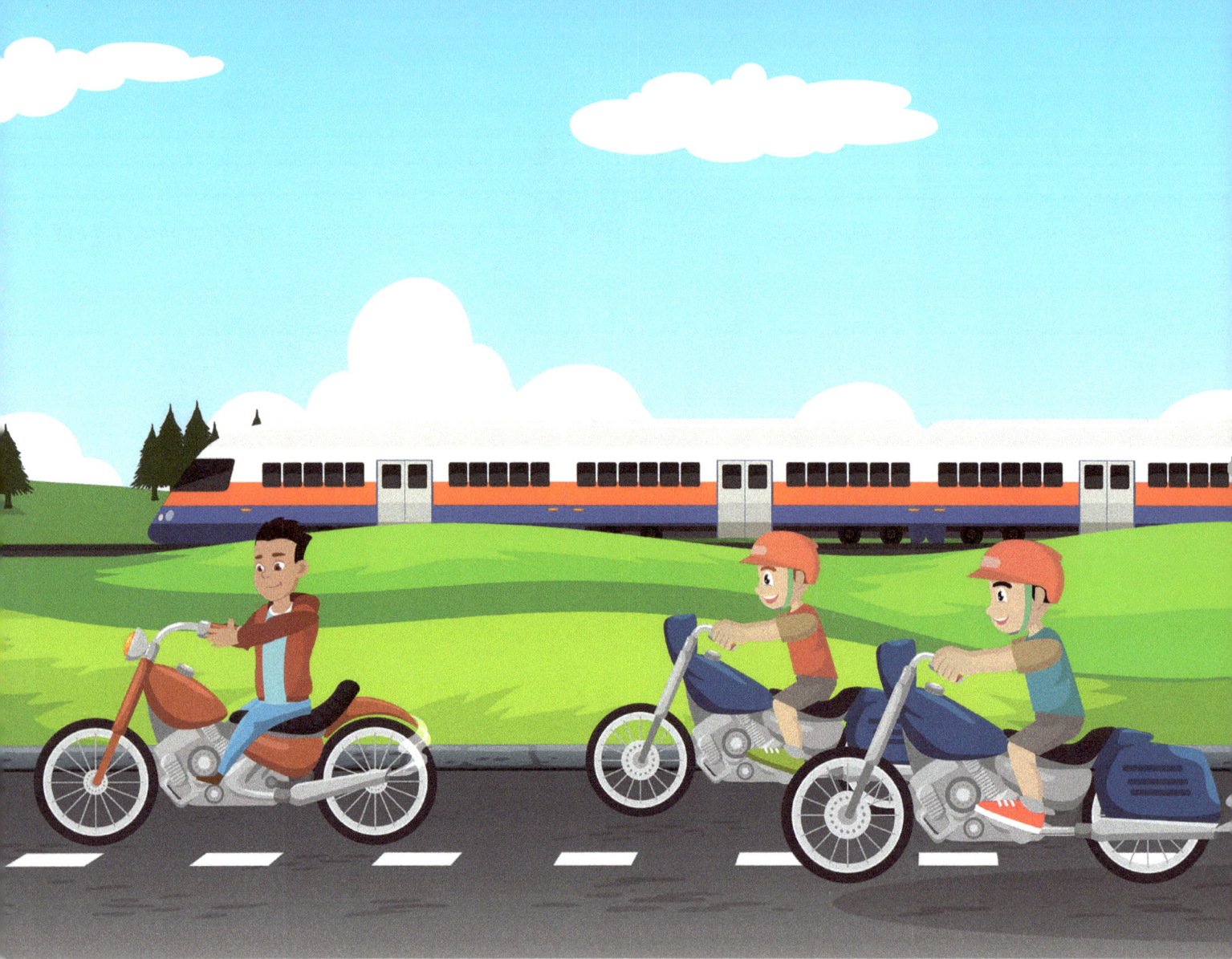

Although God is in control, a leader you can still be,

Go read what God told Moses and then read about the Red Sea.

To be a leader, you should be a person with some very thick blood.

And be a good listener, that's how Noah survived the flood.

The Bible offers food for thought, so your brain you should feed,

But if you only want a snack, Obadiah you should read.

Then share the good word with everybody, some will listen, probably not all.

Yet, you can still help spread Christianity, even if your name is not Paul.

You just need to know what you are saying, and can explain what you mean.

Don't rush people to change, be patient like King Ahasuerus when he picked Esther for Queen.

Sometimes parents will play favorites like Rebekah, but parents will do what they want to do.

Just make sure you do your part and no one will be able to steal a blessing intended for you.

Let your strength be what's in your heart, your strength is not in your hair.

Like Samson, you can lose that at any moment, so use your heart if you care.

If you wear your cross daily, there will be no storm you can't weather.

Just know the journey is easier if you have some friends like Timothy and you travel together.

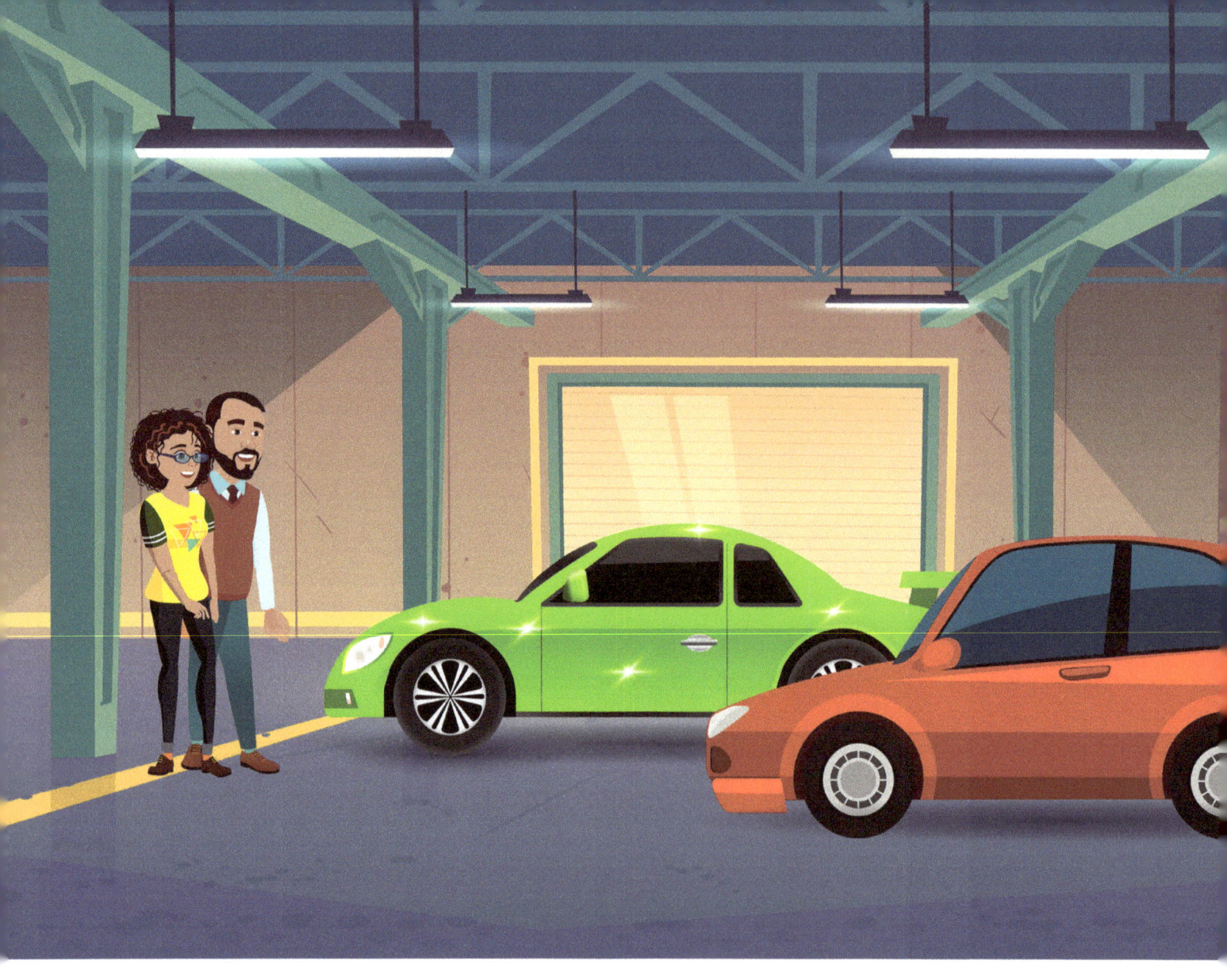

When you become successful, don't let your blessings become a curse,

Or like Uzziah getting leprosy, your life can be good and then get worse.

Having children is a blessing, but being a parent is something that can be scary.

However, there is nothing to fear if your family knows about the Son of Virgin Mary.

If you talk about your favorite topic, you will probably sound like a nerd.

How will that conversation turn out if you talked about the Word?

Hopefully you now realize that with God you can do your thing.

Let God rule your life, like the people of Persia when Xerxes was king.

You may have heard of some of these people, but some Hebrew names may be new.

Instead of talking about a spy like Yigal, this book will end by talking about You.

Remember that some days will be ugly, although like a picture, we want them all to be cute.

You should always continue to speak of God, and don't be like Zechariah when he was mute.

www.ingramcontent.com/pod-product-compliance
Lightning Source LLC
Chambersburg PA
CBHW042038100526
44587CB00030B/4475